Blood Stained Mahogany

Collin Cooper

www.PhilosophicalRambler.com

© 2021 Collin Cooper

All rights reserved. No portion of this book may be reproduced in any form without permission from the publisher, except as permitted by U.S. copyright law.

Paperback ISBN: 9798461533601

Dedicated to Humanity

Contents

Dedicated to Humanity...3

Preface..5

The Beginning...6

About the Author..185

Collin Cooper

Preface

T he following poems encapsulate an era, a story, a life. Stories have to be told; lives have to be changed. There are stories in this world that will never be told, stories that have the potential to change our perspective. Each poem is a journey, each line formed through experience. This collection includes over 170 poems, varying in length and style. The poems were written from March to August of 2021, each being unique and never before released. Words have power, there is a defining essence throughout the collection. Themes of humanity, tragedy, mortality, and humility. Expect nothing. Read every single line not only in the context of the individual piece but also in the greater perspective of what makes the first poem relate to the last. Rethink your life, consider your choices, dream your future. This existence is short, but the day is long. We all have 24 hours, make them paradise. Command your environment and take action. Move forward boldly.

Be careful, your dreams just might come true.

The Beginning

LAST PAGE

Written
On the last page of a notepad
That I have taken across the state
Many smiles
Many tears
But through it all, I kept writing…
And that is what you see here.

Going Down the Highway

Going down the highway
120 miles per hour
Viewing the surrounding reality,
As though an abstract painting.

J.E.P.

40 years without a visitor
Abounding honor
A life well lived
Because of him, you are reading
Because of him, men found
Peace in the trenches.

Eyes

Those eyes
Filled with void
Blackness indescribable,
Emotionless.

Rust

The degrading condition
Of something that someone
Once cared for.
Isn't that all of us?

PRODUCING

Producing poems
Faster than consumption
They seem to spoil
In the darkness they are kept in.

VAIN

All my efforts were in vain
It only caused me pain
But that pain allowed me to write
That which kept me awake at night.

FOREVER

Forever is but a moment
In the landscape of eternity
Joy enclosing all
Within its warm grasp
Finding peace in the toil
Finding rest in the soil
Finding a worthy cause
Underneath the sunset.

TEARS

If only our tears
Could bring them back
So alive in our hearts
The years pass by.

THE CREEK

Passing over
Over again.
The Tiber
The Nile
Those ancient waters
From which sprung life.
This creek is what we have
Flowing crystal
The throne of God.

Flawed

Aren't we all flawed at heart?
Was it this way from the start?
Or were we once whole
Enjoying life?
Now thrusting the knife
What has come upon man?
Has he become less or more?
Flaws exposed to the wind
Primitive emotion
Faces the modern world.

FADING

Shapes and colors
Fading from memory
As we abandon this world
Unwillingly.

LOST

We all seem to be lost
Like that child crying on aisle three
Looking for the direction back to safety
But our parent has left the store.

Suspended

Suspended
Atop a thin metal wire
That wire being life
Either side
Being death
Wobbling side to side
Earnestly working
To keep looking ahead
For those following the path
Of good and true
I surely must tell
This is you!

TO OBTAIN

What is there to aim for
But that which you can't obtain
With this power and force,
That you have stored inside of you.

Checkmate

Placed in a corner
Thought to be the lesser
Thought to be the fool
Thought to be the demise.
Fighting sentiment with truth
Losing self to the fire
Screams resound
Though love abounds
You will find authentic people
In the corners of this world.

IVORY

Ivory White
Simplistic Perfection
Wealth through death
Enduring strength
Forged by nature.

EGO

We've become
A novel
An ongoing story,
A feature film.

IMPOSSIBLE

What I thought was impossible
What I thought I could not do
Oh, how foolish I was
To have no faith in you
No matter what happens in this earthly life
We will see it through
Me and you.

TODAY

Looking into the abyss below
Failing to write more
Dominoes in slow motion
Inherent mental pause
Shock to the system
Ultimate deliverance
Dazed elation
Metaphysical Ocean
Road signs blown away
Maybe we still have it?
How can we know anymore?

Confinement

Internal Confinement
Inherent Joy
Pleasant Solitude
Simple Splendor
Beyond Silence
Above Rebuke
Oh, these times
We spend with ourselves.

January

Looking out the window
The world painted white
Heart beating through your head
Sipping caffeine
Surviving another day
Living on the high
Remembering year past
Entering the new
Oh, what shall come
Of this new dawn?

Glances

Glances.
Whispers.
Stares of a baby.
Taunts of the school children.
This life hasn't moved beyond the ancients, has it?

NO!

A child screams no
With the earnest of
A man,
Yet the difference is
The outcome,
Sugar and despair.

Praise

The praise
Has only created
Haze
And fueled pressure
I think we already cracked,
A long time ago.

AT LAST

Rather than feeling excitement
At that which is accomplished
One inhales a breath of fresh air,
As though on the beach.
Satisfaction.
Feeling the sun and
Rest, at last.

FORCED

Trapped inside
Four walls
How is this
Not prison?
I do not desire
To be here,
Yet,
I am,
Forced.

ANTS

Scurrying about
The designated route
They all fall into order
Just like ants.

The Greatest Pain

The greatest pain
Is inflicting despair
On those you care for.
Because what remains
Is soon gone
And so are we.
Why run
When you can barely walk?
What do you do
When you just don't know anymore?

Frozen Dominoes

Fading away
Forever shattered
Irrecuperable despair
What has come to pass
Neither money nor fame
Degree nor job
Could make you feel that way
The dominoes stopped falling
Is this the end of the game?

Conformity

The most beautiful poetry
Is written by the
Most disturbed minds
The most violent criminals were once
Innocent kids
Though the world imposes itself on you
Choose not to conform.

Continual Despair

A heart on fire
A shattered soul
Are needed to write
That which you adore,
That which makes you want more.
When you have nothing left
To explore
When your entire life has become a bore
You've bought everything
At the store
But look!
You are still crying
On the floor.

LINES AND SEASONS

How spring reminds us of fall,
All that we endured
Opportunities missed
Friends now forsaken.

NEVER

What we never said
Is what drives us to the verge of insanity.
What we never did
Because we were just kids.
Thinking about the future.

Collin Cooper

RAGGED EXISTENCE

What now do we aim for?
What now do we chase after?
What glory shall we receive?
What gold shall be given?
Is the labor not enough?
Is the toil not our friend?
Poems riddled with questions
They seem to answer themselves
Taking away pieces of our soul
Replacing them
With what we find on our journey
One does wonder how we are
Alive
With the patchwork we have done
On the wounds that never went away
Yet we made it through
The winter
So, we must be doing alright.

LURKING

Knowing what lurks
Behind that white door
As the breathing comes to a pause,
I hear a terrible screa…

Fearless

What awaits man
As the final hour
At last draws near
Oh!
What a sight!
He is not in fear!

EVERYONE IN TOWN

Looking over
At the one who made it
Who achieved that which he wanted
The guy who made it.

I Wonder

That old Camaro granddad used to own
The subject of stories, days of youthful glory
Friends who have passed on and leather worn
I wonder where it is nowadays.

THE WAY

All trying to leave a legacy
A touch
On this side of existence
Those before
Those after
What will they do?
Living with honor
Living with hope
We mustn't ask for anything more.
Hard times are coming.

Collin Cooper

PURITY

Love is one of the few things
We can grasp without sin
For divine purity is seen
In the eyes
Of those you care about.

Blood Stained Mahogany

Wealth embedded in the wood
Blood from the scars of the journey
Mixed with tears
A relic
Eternal Memories
Final thoughts
Slumber and rest
Was it peace?
Or was it death?
He was just a boy.

Collin Cooper

THE GREATEST GENERATION

Sunlight beaming through the stained glass
Reflecting on the mahogany pew
The smell of rose fills the air
Old glory in view
The people line up as a tear drops to the floor
Memories revisited
Never forgotten.

Broken Heart

A broken heart
Can take you to Paris
Writing volumes to live.
Or just reliving the pain?

LIMBO

Living in between two walls
The oxygen running out
As they slowly close in
Your heart beating faster
"Am I breathing too fast?"
Your eyes begin to flutter as the light fades into the abyss
Thud.

REFLECTION

Reflecting
On the short life that we have lived
Finding life in the breeze
Finding life in the moments
Moments that allow us to live
Moments that allow us to die.
Reflecting on possibilities,
Though you have reached the summit.
Taken for a reason
Though essence alive
A smile of peace can be found
For all those who wonder
When we look around the corner
To see them once again
Journey complete
Given all that was asked
And yet more.

Collin Cooper

ONE DAY

One day
Everyone will see
That which we have given our life for.
And what we have fought for
Will be right in front of us.

STUMBLING

Attempting to walk through hell
Stumbling about
Burdened to collapse
Pushed into the ground
Hope crucified
Dreams drowned
Somehow still walking
Somehow still breathing
Where is the end?
Give thanks for every day
You just don't know when everything will…
End.

A Wonderful Place

Trying to get back
To that sunny day
So long ago
Is what life has become.
If we do not know that day,
Then we do not know life.
What a wonderful place
Awaits.

MAYBE NOT

Maybe I am not
The person I appear to be
Because if only you could see
That which goes on inside of me
Reality would cause you to flee
Because that man you believe me to be,
I am not he.

THE LUCKY FEW

There are ten breaks for every happy ending
There are eight painful deaths for two happy lives
There are moments of suffering for all
Everyone has a story.

WORTHY

Tangerine sun
Radiating down
On the summer grass
As a man learned what he would die for.

Masquerade

You can rely on nothing in this world
Then what are we doing?
Chasing after luxury and pleasure
Running to throw ourselves into the pit
Tossing ourselves into the fire
Hoping to numb the pain
Hoping someday the story will end
For continual existence is a burden
It's time for a new actor
To take the stage once more
Oh,
This life we pretend to adore.

THE BLUES

The spirit of the blues
Running through the soul
Filling every hole
Finding every leak
Swaying
Side
To
Side
Throwing flesh and bone
Crushing dreams
Paying the bond.

Collin Cooper

Grand Idea

Started with a grand idea
At a standstill
Falling down the hill
Tumbling
Tumbling faster
Thud.
Flames surround
Those who wake
Only to consume
People already attempting to leave.

THE PIT

I've seen the bottom of the pit
There is nothing there
But a reflection
Of your life before
Now more vivid
Then you thought to be real
Twisted with pain
Consumed like taffy
You'll question everything.

RATIONAL EXPLANATION

I won't give up,
I won't cave in.
We've come too far,
I've fought too hard.
Injected with a dosage
Beyond my comprehension
Filled with emotion
Beyond rational explanation.

STEEL

Steel encapsulating
The soul within
Strangling the heart
Drowning the mind
Flowing through the veins
Consciousness starting to
Fade.

Winding Creek

Waiting for the creek
To flow to the bridge
Because that's where one can
Reflect
On the deeds they've committed
On the future they hope to have…
The possibilities of its
Failure
The chances of
Success.

Efficiency

What will we remember
In a decade from today?
Will your labor have meaning?
Who will even be there?
Will they have left you?
Or did you leave them?
We could find ourselves in
Athens
We could find ourselves in
Babylon
Primitive emotion
Prevents complete
Efficiency.

INJECTED

Alert
Awake
Aware beyond recognition
Fading coherently
Faster than the wind
Blurred kaleidoscope
Warm peach hue
Hourglass knocked over
Injected.

Sweat

Sweat flowing down the
Rusted chains
Mingled with the
Bloodstained earth

Universal Religion

The universal religion
Or was it ever?
Ruins filled with
Styrofoam beads and
Spray paint
Smoke and
Mud-stained leaves.

SCIENTIFIC GAMEPLAY

Analyzed
Dissected
Spun
Twisted
Mixed
Subtracted
Each word a move
In the grand game
Fading and appearing
Behind every alley
Temporary actors
Variable ideals
Meaningless indulgence.

TEEN

Running about
Trying all things
New
Only to feel empty
Only to feel like you
It won't end how we
Expect
When will we
Realize?
Maybe when the fires rage,
Maybe when the bayonets shimmer.

GOD'S JUDGMENT

A three-letter word
Forces man's hand
More than a sword
It forces sorrow
It forces despair
But to some
That word brought peace
That word brought joy
What did it bring you?

Man's Existence

Struggling for existence
Just to exist.
Many men caught
Without an answer for
Why they live
Thrown below
To the place they learn
What to live for.
They pay in years
Time,
Their most needed asset
At last receiving
The purchased thought
Their world ends.

PACE

Writing at the pace
Of a notebook a day
Look what has happened
Look what is yet to come!
Life is like a novel
Living a movie.

REMEDY

The bourbon won't take the memory away
When that was how you lived
Time only pulls apart the fibers of suffering
In ways we can't understand
The cigarette won't do you any good
Neither will the greenback
But that preacher man in the village down there…
He'd like to have a word with you.

THE SPECTRUM

When you've seen
Both ends of the spectrum…
To return to the middle is absurd
You wish for something more
You wish for something stronger
You wish for something higher
You wish for something lower
Because that joy you felt
You just want it again
And that pain you felt
At least it was a feeling
But now you feel nothing
And to most, that's alright
But to us, that's not an option
It's time once more to craft man anew
He won't be anything like
The man looking at you.

WATERCOLOR SKY

The sky is painted with rose
The summer wind blows through your hair
Easing all those thoughts on your weary mind
At last, freedom
Head out the window on a Saturday night
Fireflies and dreams fill the atmosphere
Unspoken words and smiles abound
When the start completes the end
Laying on the grass
Watching the stars.

REST

Say what you want
Do what you please
No,
Not a single thing will put us at ease.

Collin Cooper

PROGRESS?

Pouring these symbols
Upon Papyrus
Have we really,
Progressed?

HAZE

Tumbling into first place
Ending the race
Horizon filled with haze
Living in a continual daze
Awake all night
Thinking of moments engrained
Soul on fire
Mind in overdrive
Drunk on joy.

Collin Cooper

Suburban Silence

Peace upon
A weary mind
Silence forcing away
Despair.

Cost

Lust and pride
Greed and power
In the end
Will these make you more loved
Than a single flower?

People of the Past

People of the past
Have returned once more
The same essence that they had before.
Do you know what it's like
For prophecy to come true?
When in the end,
It all affected
You!

TRYING OUR BEST

Trying our best
As mere humans
In the never-ending spiral
The chaos
The pain.

Collin Cooper

IF

If you decided to leave
If you didn't care
If you didn't feel the same
If you lost yourself.

SO?

So the kid can write
He's got real talent
But what is he going to eat tonight?
Is the only thought on their mind
When all that he is striving for is in front of him.

Collin Cooper

WHAT IS TOMORROW?

Truth and fame
Pain and sorrow
Oh, my friend
Just wait till tomorrow.

Defeated

You don't realize
You hit someone who is
Defeated
Only causing
Agony
Great as
Crucifixion.

Collin Cooper

HONOR

To live with
Honor
Is all a man must do
Yet when I
Look around
I see
Very few.

CREDENTIALS

A broken heart,
A troubled mind,
Is this not the start,
Where we all began?

Hoping to Write

Sitting

Waiting for the stream of inspiration

Hoping by chance you can write

Ya' know? Write something real good

Something that'll get you the luxury of the dollar menu

Something that'll keep you rambling another day

Something that will make your name known.

I May Be Wrong

I may be wrong.
Maybe I have fallen for a con
A trick
A brutally sinister joke.
Maybe…you have to
And maybe you have also felt
That of which I speak

Rip Current

Living in retrospect
Swept under the ocean of thought
Mind on fire
Yet, soul at peace
Taking gulps of saltwater
Is your final moment
Fading away
Into the ocean
Once more.

NEIGHBORHOOD

Neighborhood.
A perimeter
Of the system
That encloses
All things.

BLACK EYES

Even a saint
Can admire the devil
For whatever he can decipher
In his flowing black eyes.

MATERIAL

Is material
Abundance
What men
Died for?
Or rather a story?
In the times of old.

Collin Cooper

Taken

Isolation is a reaction
When the mind
Goes numb
When the heart
Goes cold
When they were
Taken.

The Answer

Life viewed in perspectives
Enmeshed complexities
Toppling inherent simplicity
Hoping to find the answer.

Surely I've Lived

I've traveled the world
Yet you won't find a passport
I've talked with the greatest
Yet you won't find their footprint
I've died more than I've lived
Yet you won't find a gravestone…
Surely, I've lived.

NOTHING

What is left now?
Nothing
What can you do with
Nothing?
Can you sell it?
Can you live it?
Can you kill it?
Can you write it?
Well…
Can you love it?

Deepest Sorrow

The deepest sorrow
Can be found in
The greatest joy
For all we endure,
All connects together
In the end.

NOVEL

Life like a novel
Each hour a day
Each day a week
Each week an eternity
Only for me?
Since all has come to pass
How it was
Supposed to be?

Distorted Elation

Distorted elation
Further retraction
Deeper seclusion.
Silence.
What is to come?
Already done?
Why write anymore?
The novel continues
We cling to it
Please don't let it end.

The Beginning

That ground
Brushed with sunshine
Reflected in our smiles
Watered by our tears
It hasn't changed
Through the years
But we have changed…
It's no longer the same.
That place that was special,
That place where it all began.

Dead Man's Pleasure

Walking on…
Concealing pain with pleasure
Clouding grief with intoxication
Bludgeoning the past with the present
Watching the self crumble
Fading away…

Veiled Despair

The fear of losing
What was recently gained
A pain of the soul
A plague on the mind
Deeper than I knew
Nihilistic at the core,
Christian sanity.
Religious triumph
Or
Veiled despair?

Collin Cooper

YIELD

Striking a barren rock
Fresh waters do flow
The mind yields
What is needed for all
So, wait and make it through
You'll see another day
Just need to remember who
And that in the end
Will lead back to you.

HOW ARE YOU?

How are you?
I'm alright
What about you?
I'm holding on…
The conversation drops.
We don't ask
What could make them better
We don't ask
What could make them happy
We just keep walking
Forgetting we even spoke
Just another face
Another voice
Another human.
How are you?

Collin Cooper

PLEASE REALIZE

If we never reach what was expected of us
Please realize that isn't what we were trying to be…
If we never get the house, if we never get the car,
Please realize we have something greater
Holding us together at the seams.

HOMELAND

Sweat and toil
Brown dirt mixed with clay
Green weighted grass,
Long overgrown.

NOTEPAD

Lines
Stacked upon each other
Is that how they
Are meant to be?
Or is this about us?
And what our lives have come to be?
Or maybe it's about YOU
And all you've done.
All you meant to do…
All you never did.
Those regrets
Those sleepless nights
Parasites on the soul.

USED TO

Can a style be forever?
A smile meant to last
A faded rose
Found pressed in an old book
Printed 1910.

Relative Objectivity

Relative Objectivity
Subject to Euphoria
Affected by drunken delusions
Changed by rapid growth.
Visibly incoherent
Grandeur to one
What a splendid world
Man has crafted.

SEEMS TO ME

Seems to me
In this world today
We can't find what we
Tend to be looking for
And yet we keep searching
We keep fighting
Hoping maybe it'll turn up
Like a pair of lost car keys
But that car is our life
And inside of that car is a newly purchased
Tank of gas
But we can't seem to find those keys
So, we keep on searching.

Hospital Room

Sitting in a hospital room
Laughing free and clear
Moments before you learn…
The person has died next door.
So, your voice goes low
But there is still a grin on your face.
As the wailing cries grow
You say, "Oh well, that's how life goes"
Why it has to be like this,
Nobody knows.

LUCID DREAMS

14-hour days
10-hour nights
Floating along
Dissecting dream from life
Thus, life from dream
Are they different at all?
Why not include them together?
We are human after all…

Wooden Chair

Sitting in an old wooden chair
Writing poems
Nobody will probably ever read
Then who is this for?
You best decide.
Because I don't know the answer myself
But you probably do
You know…
It's right in front of you.

Snapshot

The stack of books
Sitting on my shelf
They bear my name
But what about my heart?
For that was a snapshot in time…
I've grown a lot.

Beige Summer

Summer has
Affected the hourglass
The clock seems to have added time
Or have I just begun to live?
Or have I just begun to die?
I'm not sure there is a reason why.

Cohesive

Finding prophecy fulfilled?
An odd feeling of being
Cohesive
Silly putty
Holding together an
Appearance
Forged in tears
Refreshed continually by
Money

Collin Cooper

BACK THEN

What you wrote one week ago
Yeah, that long ago
Back then
Back when?
When did that time exist?
Did that time ever exist?
Why is this something
In my mind?

DISTORTED CULTURE

Signing a piece of paper
Who knew that matter affected the soul?
We all knew soul affected matter
Or did we?
Some of us still don't
Or do they?
Has the metal become
Too loud?
Oh no,
That's just culture.

Collin Cooper

From the Depths

Turning up the volume
Is it 100 degrees in here?
Why is the sky moving?
Red blurs with white
Turquoise entering the scene
Bountiful yellow
Neon green
Purple
Blackout.

Psychedelic Tears

Gliding along the train tracks
Falling through the ceiling of the abbey
Shot by a man in blue.
Was that not all reflected
When we look at each other?
Or was that just to me
Why is the man in the tree?
What is he doing there?
Oh.

OPEN CRIME SCENE

Youthful existence
Grown into
An open crime scene
People take what they want
There are no police
Yellow tape blown away
Not recovered.
Walking, though
Unstable
The bullet is found.

WOOD AND STEEL

No please sir!
A child!
Oh, look!
It is now a child!
Oh, the poor creature!
Oh, the little devil!
His father was a tyrant!
Hm, madame?
Thud.

NAUSEA

Strobe lights
Vodka
Punk rock
2003
Delirium
Confusion
Momentum
Black synthetic material.

PARTITIONED

Each square
Partitioned
Each square
Sold
Grass and gasoline
Wood and aluminum
Man's shack for existence
His supposed castle.

Collin Cooper

Unending Time

Years compounded
Weeks expanded
Life unchanging
Continuing personal hibernation
Waiting longer
Waiting for reveal.
Fermenting and
Twisting
Genius into existence
Art into being
Words into life.

COMMUNICATE

To talk
To share
To speak
Words forging ideas
You wouldn't comprehend
Can I say that
I do?
I'm still working,
Always will be.
That's why I wanted to
Communicate.
But will you?
That expression is enough
To understand all
Or is it?

SICKNESS

Sickness brought by an
Overloaded mind
Overloaded heart
Overloaded soul.
Now it is time to live
Larger,
That's why I'm here.

NEGATIVITY

Comprehensive negativity
Fulfilled by positivity
Blown apart mentality
When it all comes true
When it all ends
For you.

Beauty

There is inherent beauty
In majestic simplicity
Naturally crafted
Undefined
Unrefined
A rose under the sunset
Made out of glass.

SUBSTITUTE

Ambition counterfeited for
Love
A potent distraction yet a
Powerful illusionary drug
Blurring the vision of the
Refined Soul
One who thought to be
Mature.

PRODUCTION

Production of art
The despair of man
Excruciating removal
Enjoyment by the mass
Enjoyment in pain?
Enjoyment in communal despair?
Aren't you reading this?

VOLUNTARY HELL

Screaming acceptance
Voluntary hell
Living for enjoyment
As the sun glares
The alcohol flows
Overrun mortal beings
Wishing to go to
Hell.

Collin Cooper

EXHAUSTED WORDS

If only we could make
More words
For I am running out of
Ways to tell you
How I feel
Ways to tell you
How you should feel
Or is that what I am doing
At all?

FORTH

Memories spring forth
When we think about those days
Eternity smiled
As the sun glittered,
Memories come forth
Every Christmas
Every 4th of July
What could have been?

WOULD HAVE

They would have
Been proud.
You know they would have.
Because they were there for it all
When no one else believed.
When no one else would have.
You know they would have.
You know they would have.
Because they are watching you now.

2017

Fading memories
Played till the tape
Broke.
Rerecording over the past
Forging a new narrative
A new story
It is over.

71621

Materialistic delirium
Heaven and hell divided
By a razor blade
That sometimes breaks.

AFFIRMATIVE

Breathing the music
Concentrated in your being
Your hopes
Your stress
Seem to follow the beat
When the world turns against you
It may seem to be all that is left
It'll lift you up
Because you need to keep moving
Tears will drown you quickly.

Collin Cooper

SHY

When society takes
The world from you
When it promised you gain
What have you been doing
With your entire life?
Devoted to a lie
An illusion
That shatters when you
Attempt to release
Your soul.

APPEAR

Soon we will all
Appear
And soon we will all
See them again
Because they are still alive
Though we don't remember
And pretend not to care
And pretend not to care.
Remember they will
One day appear.

Collin Cooper

Illusionary Jump

Jumping out of the window
As the rusted revolver fired
Cushioned by materials
Enough to forget what
To live for.

INVISIBLE POWERS

They rule over this land
Your mind
Your body
Why are they amongst us?
Why do they stare from
Across the room?
Why do they look at us
Through mirrors
Why is it standing
Behind you?

Collin Cooper

Victorian Funeral

Wrapped in black finery
Polished ivory statues stand
The words are spoken
As though out of a speaker
The regimental flag
Is the shroud of choice
A fallen young man
In his homeland's service.

To Pass

Choking gasps of oxygen
Mixed with the terror
In the eyes of the unrepentant officer
As the red wave swept across the land
Honor and tradition trampled
She has fallen.

Rambling Seeker

Psych music flows from his
Handheld CD player
His hair unwashed for two weeks
Shines in the humid afternoon sun
Sipping a cup of
Modern gourmet coffee
From a specialty café
Smiling at the children
Who pass him by.

FOUNDATIONAL CRACK

When that which you care for
Is taken
Is taken again
Is taken by society
Is taken once more
What does the world expect
The reaction to be
When there is now a
Foundational Crack
When there is a fading memory
Of what just was
Of what just was to be
Oh, remember me
Remember me
Though I will pass by
A visitor.

DEATH BLOW

Oh, sir
He is already stumbling
Please!
Do not use that
Whip in your hand
Oh, cruel world
You have pushed him
Hard enough
His wish was to
Fade away
Yet he is brought to
Vivid reality
The blood flows
Not stopping from
Words.
Did words ever help us?
Or was it the smile?
The laughter?
We aren't here long.

The Rise and Fall

Soon you will have
Pulled enough cards out of the deck
To get to the point you are at now
Soon you will pull another card
Soon you will.
That card won't help
It'll undo you from the core
It will lead you to despair
But if we don't pull any more cards
We can't expect anything better to happen
Expecting fate
Tearing up the soul.
Lord, why does it have to be this way?

Lifetime of Reflection

Words lead to
A lifetime of reflection
Because what else can a man do
When all he cared about fell through
Our tears can't repair
The hole that is within
When that hole will never go away
Trying to live…
It wasn't meant to be this way.

June

Smiles fade to tears
Knowing how few understand
The throbbing soul
So many of us carry inside
Bearing the burden
The best we can.
Asking God
Why we are the chosen few.

Collin Cooper

GIVEN

Given the cards
With no option
So little time
That is even less lived
A forced hand
Eternal consequences
An answered prayer
A promise
A wish
It all came true.

A Reservation in Hell

A reservation in hell
Delayed by golden chains
Society today
This land we call our own
We might as well drink to
The end of what we knew
The Athenians never died out.

WINK

Passing by on the street
Catching the wink of a passerby
Is there a plot to the story?
Maybe the red light never died out
Is this the rise?
Maybe the barrier
Collapsed
Drinking champagne
Diamonds sparkle in the moonlight.

SATURATED CIVILITY

Praising virtuous toxicity
Eating dollar signs
Customized caskets going 120
Pink and blue blur into
Childhood cotton candy
Waking up alive in the
ER.
What are we doing Saturday night?

Collin Cooper

MEADOW

Tears blur the pieces that are left
Of the shattered soul
That will never recover.
Milestones pass by
As the heart can no longer bear
The pain it has to carry.
Words won't fill the hole
The wound
The burden.

THE WRITERS PEN

What the sword could not accomplish
The pen swiftly finished
What the pen could not tell
A smile promptly filled
Humanity places its faith in
Tears and words,
Truth.

Collin Cooper

MUD

Mud absorbs the fallen
Without discrimination for
Dreams and kindness
Attempting to reverse
The rapid descent
Survivors aren't the same
Yet expected to be stronger
They reply,
Fine.

Legend

"Ah, what a legend in the making!"
You've seen a legend?
"Genius!"
You've met one?
"Artist!"
You've lived like one?
"Writer!"
You are one?

❧

CLOUDY DAY

Sometimes on those
Cloudy days
Life becomes too much
For a damaged heart to handle.
Sometimes on those
Cloudy days
We forget about the sun
Because it doesn't look
Like it will ever come back.

SOBER

Sobered emotional neutrality
A world of grey winter
Trudging along through the snow
Barefoot.

Collin Cooper

Tangerine Windowpane

Clouded glass reflecting the sun of
Caesar
Reflecting the
Heroic misery
That seems to never go away
Rotating musical chairs
Revolve around the mind
Leaving the passerby in
The agony of realism.

THANKS?

The thanks we get yesterday
Is the pain of today
The chilling winds
Eroding the soul
The knock at the door in
Sixty years' time.

DEFICIENCY

Deficiency funneling
Creative ability
Existence enhanced
Transformative curse.

PHYSICAL FORCE

Physical Force
Starts where the
Thought ends
When logic falls away
When emotions go into
Overdrive.

❦

Collin Cooper

Rotating Fame

Rotating fame
Enhances the story
Flavors the movie
What is expected?
Building you up
To find a fault.
Public sacrifice
Never went away.

Trading Time

Trading time for
A logo
Material yet important
To you?
Or the world?
Time seems to run out
Can't we print more?

Collin Cooper

SKETCH

Sketching the idea
Rudimentary words
Forging pictures of wind
Blowing away the memories
We try to hold onto,
Creating.

Glitter

Tread at a wedding in May
At the last vacation in July
It fell off at the funeral in the
December snow.

They Think

They think
They think you are.
They think you are…
Happy
Successful
Wealthy
Proud.
But what was the price to you?
You took your past
And threw it overboard.

Us

Though we walk
Upon the same concrete
The only thing that
Changed
Was us.

Collin Cooper

INCOHERENT

Incoherent whispers
Inside a dream
Reminding you
Where to go,
What to do
Eroding away
Remembering the directions.

RED WINE

Red wine
Leading to silver platters
Leading to green grass
Cobblestone and
FIRE!

Collin Cooper

BENEATH THE **G**REEN

Beneath the green
At peace?
They lay
Arms folded and eyes closed
Draped in
Red
White
And Blue.

Impending Thunder

Slamming a fist full of aces on the table
The players stand in shock
Until a chuckle is heard
Laughter roars from all
A revolver is seen
A spade follows.

POMPEII

Entangled in cobwebs
As the volume is turned up
The party before
Pompeii.

APPEARANCES

Keeping up
On the gold-plated treadmill
With hands tied up in platinum
Shoes filled with lead
When will you
Collapse?

Fashion

Homeless using
Discarded Saks bags
To carry around
Their daily bread.

Faster

Live happier
Live larger
Live wealthier
Live faster.

Collin Cooper

Nothing Wrong

When you did
Nothing wrong
It makes defeat much sweeter
When you did nothing wrong
You realize
Too much honey is
Toxic.

Molten

Fiery burdens
We do hold in our hands
Hiding them away in our soul
Molten.

The End

About the Author

Collin Cooper is a Philosopher, Poet, Amazon Bestselling Author, Apologist, and so much more. His work has been read by thousands in over 50 countries. He writes on the blog "Philosophical Rambler." He resides in Carmel, Indiana and is currently pursuing further traditional education.

Made in the USA
Monee, IL
22 October 2021